Child Support in Canada

What everyone ought to know

Table of Contents

Preliminaries

- Paying Child Support
- Lawyers & Child Support
- Mothers & Child Support
- Parents Living Abroad
- Surprise Pregnancy

Child Support Guidelines

- Child Support Amount
- Calculating Income
- Paying More
- Paying Less
- Summer Stays
- Life Insurance Requirements
- Extended Health & Dental Benefits
- Taxation of Child Support
- Use of Child Support
- Access Denied
- Visitation Denial
- Unmarried Parents
- Paying in Cash
- Split Custody
- Shared Custody
- Determination of 40% Threshold
- How Much Child Support if There is Shared Custody
- Special or Extraordinary Expenses
- Spousal Support
- Retroactive Child Support
- Private Schooling
- Payments to the Child
- Previous Relations & Child Support Payments
- Food & Clothing Credit
- Unmatched Parental Income
- Undue Hardship
- Cost of Child Support
- Overseas Calculations
- Taxes & Cost of Living
- Child Support for Adult Children
- Child Support Tables

Determining Income

- Income for Child Support
- Self Employment
- Low Paying Job
- Income Fluctuations
- Overtime & Bonuses
- Capital Gains & Losses
- Large One Time Capital Gain
- Remarriage
- Earning Power vs Actual Earnings

Adult Children

- College / University Age
- Amounts Paid
- Child's Income
- Post Secondary Education Expenses
- Lack of Communication
- Working / Returning To School

StepChildren

- Paying Requirements
- Deciding Factors
- Two Fathers

Separation Agreements

- Understanding the Agreement
- Acceptance by the Judge
- Difference from the Guidelines
- Varying Child Support

Variation of Child Support

- Locked In Agreement
- Changing Support
- Retroactive Support
- Arrears Calculations
- Retirement
- Reduction of Arrears
- Remarriage
- Layoff
- Wage Garnishment

Termination of Child Support

- Ending Time
- Quitting School
- No Graduation

Enforcement of Child Support Orders

- Payroll Deductions
- Payment Enforcement
- Collecting Outside Canada
- Family Responsibility Office
- Enforcing Support
- Bypassing the Agency
- Wage Garnishment
- Interest on Unpaid Support

Document Disclosure

- Normal Documentation
- Self-Employment Documentation
- Nondisclosure

Miscellaneous Issues

- New Discovery
- Bankruptcy
- Legal Fees
- Interim Child Support

Child Support in Canada

Preliminaries

To get started, we need to start at the very beginning, which is determining whether child support even needs to be paid. The first question people ask is, "Do I have to pay child support?"

Paying Child Support

Without hesitation, if you are the non-custodial parent or if your child does not reside primarily with you, then by law, you are required to pay child support.

The law views child support to be a right of your children. It is not a right of the parents. The money is intended to be there to contribute to your children's care and maintenance.

Once parents are living in different residences, an obligation to pay child support automatically arises, regardless of whether there is an agreement or court order to pay child support. (There are limits to how far back a court will go in awarding child support, which I will discus later).

Lawyers and Child Support

You do not necessarily need a lawyer to get child support. You and the other parent may well be able to agree on an appropriate amount of child support between yourselves, particularly where your financial situation is straightforward (for instance, where the parent paying child support is a salaried employee).

A mediator or some other neutral third party may also be of assistance in finalizing details of an agreement, particularly if you and your ex-partner have difficulty communicating.

As well, if the only issue involved in your case is child support, it is a fairly straightforward matter to prepare the paperwork necessary to apply to the court for a child support order. Contrary to what many people believe, you have the right to represent yourself in court. Courts in many provinces have information centres located at the courthouse where you can obtain the necessary paperwork and get help filling it out. Or, you may simply attend at a lawyer's office for a consultation, and have the lawyer explain to you how to do this.

There are certain types of child support cases that are more complicated, and for which you should at least consult with a lawyer. The first of these is if you are a step-parent who is being requested to pay child support. A second type of case is where you parent your children over 40% of the time. A third type of case is where your "child" is over the age of majority. Finally, if the support payor is self-employed, it can be complicated to determine exactly what income should be used for child support purposes.

Mothers and Child Support

The Child Support Guidelines do not discriminate between men and women. This means that if the mother is the non-custodial parent or if the children do not reside with her for the majority of time, then just as with the father, she is required to pay child support. The same is true for step-mothers and mothers in same-sex relationships.

Parents Living Abroad

As long as your children are resident in Canada, it is the Canadian child support laws that apply.

A parent living abroad continues to be bound by child support orders or agreements so long as the children are resident in Canada. This means that the parent living abroad must continue to pay the agreed or ordered amount in Canadian dollars regardless of where he or she is living.

If the parent living abroad is not making child support payments as ordered or agreed, the custodial parent can get assistance with enforcing payment of child support. There are many reciprocal support enforcement agreements between Canada, its provinces and other countries, which allow for the enforcement of orders made in Canadian jurisdictions in foreign countries.

There are also government agencies that deal with this particular problem. These services include tracing parents who have defaulted on their child support, suspending federal licenses and passports of parents who are not meeting child support obligations, and garnishing or intercepting federal payments that would go to parents who are not paying child support.

Surprise Pregnancy

Sadly, some people become parents because they have been lied to. For example, it is not uncommon to hear stories about women lying about taking the pill, only to surprise an uninterested party that he is about to become a father.

Regardless of how you became a parent, you are required to pay child support. Canada's Child Support Guidelines is based on parenthood, whether the child is a result of a long-term relationship or a one-night stand.

Child Support Guidelines

In this chapter, I discuss some important aspects of the Child Support Guidelines. This will provide you with a much better idea of exactly what your legal rights and obligations are.

Child Support Amount

The big question on everyone's mind is, "How much child support will I have to pay or will I receive?"

The amount of child support you are required to pay is based on tables that are a part of the Child Support Guidelines. These tables can be found at Justice.gc.ca.

The tables use a formula based on the cost of living and provincial income tax to determine the amount of child support a person must pay. Additionally, the amounts in the Child Support Guidelines are based on average amounts that families spend to care for their children nationally.

The two primary factors in determining the amount of child support you must pay is your annual income and the number of children you are paying child support for.

You are pretty much required to follow the tables. For instance, if you and the other parent agree on an amount significantly different from the table amount of child support, the other parent can simply go to court and get this changed. As well, a judge will not grant a divorce if the amount of child support varies from the table amount significantly without there being a good reason for this.

Calculating Income

The most controversial question in most child support cases is exactly how much income the person paying support is earning. In fact, I have devoted an entire chapter to this topic.

One confusing aspect of income when it comes to child support is whether net or gross income should be used – the answer is gross income. For most people, this will be the figure you entered on line 150 of your T1 General Tax Return.

Paying More

You may be required to pay more than the table amount of child support.

The amount of child support in the child support tables is just a base amount. In addition to the table amount, the court may add amounts for special expenses, such as day care or child care, special extra-curricular activities, special educational expenses, or medical, health, dental or orthodontal expenses not covered by health insurance plans.

The after-tax cost of these special expenses is shared between the two parents in proportion to their incomes. The after-tax aspect is important as many special expenses, such as child care expenses, are also tax deductible.

Paying Less

There are also situations when you may be able to pay less than the table amount of child support. Examples of this are when there is shared custody or undue hardship.

Undue hardship exists when there exists factors that make it difficult for you to pay the table amount of child support. The factors must somehow arise out of the relationship itself, such as debts incurred to support your family before you separated, unusually high access costs to visit your children, or a legal obligation to pay child or spousal support to someone else.

In addition to this, you must also show that paying the table amount of child support would mean you have a lower standard of living than your ex-partner.

In addition, the Divorce Act does recognize some special circumstances that may also result in less child support being ordered by a judge. Circumstances such as transfer of property or investments may reduce your child support as the transfer may be considered financially in lieu of child support payments. For instance, you may gratuitously transfer your share of the matrimonial home to your spouse so that your spouse can remain there with your children. In this case, you'd most likely be entitled to a reduction in child support.

Another reason to pay a lesser amount of child support is if you and the other parent have shared custody. Shared custody means that both of you have custody, plus you each spend approximately equal amounts of time with the children. Note that shared custody does not automatically entitle you to reduce your child support payments. You must show that your increased costs of parenting the children for more time, and the other parent's decreased costs of parenting the children for less time merits a decrease in child support.

In making an order for child support that is less than the table amount, it is required by law that the judge include a written statement detailing the reasons why a lesser amount is being paid.

Summer Stays

If you are the parent paying child support and your child or children stay with you for an entire summer, you are still required to pay child support during the summer. The reason for this is that the custodial parent still has a lot of the normal expenses for raising the children even though the children are not there – for instance, maintaining a larger home and car.

However, there may be mitigating circumstances that help you out with these payments. The so-called "40 percent" rule is one way that you can reduce your payments. If your children are with you for 40 percent of each year, approximately 146 days, then you might qualify to be considered for "shared custody."

Life Insurance Requirements

Life insurance, with the other parent the beneficiary in trust for your child or children, is normally required in a child support agreement or court order.

This is to protect your children in the unlikely even that you should pass away prior to your child support obligation ending. Because of this, it is normal for both parents to obtain life insurance – even the parent who is not paying child support.

If the specified insurance were not purchased, and you should pass away, then your estate would still have a child support obligation. As well, many agreements provide that the other parent has a first charge on your estate for the amount of life insurance that was supposed to be in place.

Therefore, it is in your best interests to comply with the child support agreement when it calls for you to take out a life insurance policy.

Extended Health and Dental Benefits

Your child support agreement or court order will normally require you to provide extended health or dental benefits for your children if these are available to you at a reasonable cost through your employment. Just remember that the premiums required for these benefits are not considered a part of your child support payment.

Taxation of Child Support

The tax status of your child support payments depends entirely on when you negotiated your child support agreement or when the courts issued a child support court order. If you negotiated child support agreements after May 1, 1997, your child support payments are not tax deductible. This is because on May 1, 1997, new Child Support Guidelines were brought into effect that canceled a previous tax deduction.

The rationale behind this was that separated couples were accessing a tax loophole not available to other Canadians. Since the payee was usually in a lower tax bracket, he or she would generally pay income tax at a lower rate on the additional income, while the payor could reduce his or her income and pay less tax at the higher rate.

By ensuring that the payor paid income tax on child support payments, the government ensured that the provincial and federal governments were able to collect income tax on every dollar earned and that the payee was able to apply the entire child support payment to help their child or children.

In the case of agreements negotiated before May 1, 1997, the payor is able to deduct the child support payments from his or her total income. The payee is then required to claim the child support payments as income, and pay the applicable federal and provincial income tax.

If your agreement was negotiated before May 1, 1997, you are covered by a grandfather clause, which allows you to continue using this tax loophole. However, if you or the other parent would prefer agree to use the new tax system, then you have the option of petitioning the court to have the tax status of your current agreement changed to match the tax status set out in Canada's Child Support Guidelines (or updated to reflect the Guidelines amount).

Use of Child Support

Many parents have concern that the money they are paying toward child support is not being used properly. Unfortunately, once the order for child support payments is in place, you will have absolutely no control over how the child support is used.

The reason for this is that the court presumes that since the custodial parent is responsible enough to care for the child or children, he or she is also responsible enough to apply the child support payments appropriately in caring for the child or children.

The only part of child support payments that must be specifically directed are the special or extraordinary expenses called for in Section Seven of you're the Child Support Guidelines. These expenses cover things like child care, extended health or dental benefits, and educational expenses.

Access Denied

Another huge concern for divorced parents is that they will be denied access to their child but still be required to pay child support. There are absolutely no circumstances under which you can unilaterally decide to stop paying child support, even if your former partner is denying you access to your children.

Only a judge can decide whether you should be allowed to stop paying child support, and even in cases of curtailed access the courts have shown a tremendous reluctance to do this. If you are being denied access to your children, your first course of action should be to petition a family court to have your access order enforced.

A judge will then decide whether your access order has been breached, and will order your partner to comply with the terms of that agreement. Although it may be frustrating to have to take this action, it is better to do things the right way than to irritate the court by breaching the terms of your child support order.

Visitation Denial

You cannot deny visitation just because you have not received child support payments. Even if you have not received child support payments for several months, you are still required to comply with the terms of your access order.

Although this may seem unfair, the purpose of this requirement is to prevent children from getting in the middle of a fight over child support. The governments of Canada and of all the provinces have agreed that it is important to try to foster good relationships between non-custodial parents and their children.

Therefore, your violating an access order or agreement will be seen not as a step to ensure the other partner pays up but as an attempt to prevent the fostering of that good relationship. Now keep in mind that you can get help from the government and the courts to collect your child support. Additionally, there are reciprocal agreements in place with other countries if the other parent lives abroad.

Unmarried Parents

You are responsible for child support for any child you have had, whether you married the other parent or not. Your child support will be determined by provincial statutes which are based on the federal Child Support Guidelines.

If the child's paternity is disputed, you may be required to take a biological test to determine if you are the father. If you are, you will be ordered to pay child support – it is as simple as that.

Paying in Cash

It is extremely inadvisable to pay your child support in cash, because there would then be no record of the transaction. With no record of the transaction, you will then be vulnerable to a claim from the other parent that you never actually made the child support payment at all.

In most cases you can arrange for your bank to transfer funds directly to your spouse's account, or you can provide a series of post-dated cheques each year. Either of these methods will ensure that you have an adequate record of the child support you have paid.

Generally, your child support agreement or court order will specify exactly how you are to pay your child support, and you should follow these instructions to the letter.

Split Custody

In the event that each parent has custody of at least one child, this is called "split custody." The amount of child support to be paid in situations of split custody is calculated by determining the amount that each parent would be required to pay under the Child Support Guidelines if a child support claim was made against them.

The parent who would have had to pay the higher amount is then required to pay the difference between the two child support table amounts. They will still also be required to pay a portion of any special or extraordinary expenses.

Shared Custody

If your child spends significant time with you as the non-custodial parent, then yes, your child support payments can be reduced if your children spend more than 40 percent of each year with you. Known as shared custody, there are special provisions in the federal Child Support Guidelines that govern these situations.

Determination of 40% Threshold

There's no fixed formula for determining the 40% threshold. Different judges have done it differently in different cases. In some cases, the judges look at hours, in other cases, the judges look at days, in still other cases, the judges look at overnights, and sometimes other approaches are used.

In general however, to be able to argue that you should have a reduction in child support due to shared custody, it must be fairly clear that you parent the children 40 percent of the time. If it is debateable whether you have reached the 40 percent threshold, even if you are successful in convincing a judge that you have reached the threshold, you are not likely to get much of a break in child support.

Note that additional time you spend with your children over summer vacations and holidays is counted in determining the 40 percent threshold – not just the regular access schedule.

How Much Child Support if there is Shared Custody

Another question often asked is, "If there is shared custody, what is my child support reduced to?" There are no hard and fast rules which determine the amount of child support payable in shared custody situations. The federal Child Support Guidelines state that:

> "Where a spouse exercises a right of access to, or has physical custody of, a child for not less than 40 per cent of the time over the course of a year, the amount of the child support order must be determined by taking into account:
>
> - The amounts set out in the applicable tables for each of the spouses
> - The increased costs of shared custody arrangements; and
> - The conditions, means, needs, and other circumstances of each spouse and of any child for whom support is sought."

What this means is that in a shared custody situation, the judge can use his or her own discretion when deciding how much child support will be awarded. He or she will weigh all of the factors listed in the guidelines when deciding the amount.

A court order for child support in a shared custody situation will normally be accompanied by a statement declaring the reasons why the court has decided on the particular amount of child support payable.

If you are reluctant to leave this decision entirely in the hands of the courts, you can and should try to reach an agreement with the other parent before the court issues the child support order. If you are able to submit a proposal that is acceptable to both parties, the court will generally accept this amount.

Note that even if you and the other parent look after your children the exact same amount of time, you will like still be required to pay child support, if your income is significantly higher than the other parent's income.

Special or Extraordinary Expenses

Many different expenses can be considered special and extraordinary, and it really depends on the unique needs of your child or children. In general, these expenses include:

- Child care or daycare expenses required by the custodial parent's employment, disability, or educational program
- Health related expenses, such as cosmetic surgeries, orthodontic work, psychological counselling, physiotherapy, speech therapy, drug costs, glasses or other vision aids, and hearing aids if necessary
- Extended health or dental care premiums
- Educational aides, tutors, and other special assistance for primary and secondary school students as needed
- Post-secondary education costs (college, trade school, or university)
- Any expenses for school, religious-based, or other recreational activities

Shared

Parents share special or extraordinary expenses in proportion to their incomes. For example, if one parent made $20,000 and the other $60,000, the first parent would pay one quarter of the (after tax cost of the) expense, while the second would pay the remaining 75 percent.

If the child is over the age of majority, both parents would pay their respective portions of the expense after first subtracting contributions made by the child (such as savings used to help pay for university) and any grants, bursaries, or other subsidies the child may receive.

While the proportional rule is the usual guide for courts, the parents may agree on different amounts and present that agreement to the court. For instance, if both parents earn approximately the same amount, the costs are often shared 50/50, rather than determining the exact percentage that each parent should pay.

Spousal Support

If you are paying spousal support in addition to child support, you can deduct the amount of spousal support paid from your total income before your share of any special and extraordinary expenses is calculated. Similarly, the other parent would add on the spousal support they are receiving in calculating their share of any special or extraordinary expenses.

However, you may not deduct spousal support payments from the income used to determine your basic child support payments.

Retroactive Child Support

Your obligation to pay child support technically commences immediately upon separation. As a practical matter your child support obligation will only commence when you and your spouse physically separate, so long as you continue to pay your share of the household expenses while you're living under the same roof with your spouse.

In awarding child support, a court normally will not go back more than a year before child support was originally requested, unless there is a good reason to do so (for instance, there was difficulty in locating the child support payor).

Private Schooling

In most cases, unless the parents are very wealthy, a private school would be considered a special and extraordinary expense, in which case both parents would pay a proportional share of the costs based on their total incomes (after taking into account any income tax deductions).

Typically, it is best for both parents to agree on the expenses that will be applicable to the child in question. However, if parents cannot agree whether an expense is necessary, it will be up to the judge to determine the "necessity and reasonableness" of the expense.

There are several factors that go into this decision, one of which is a standard of living. If your ex-spouse is trying to significantly increase the standard of living that you had prior to separation, a judge can decide it is not essential for you to contribute to the expense of a private school.

To make such a determination, the judge will look at factors such as your family spending habits before separation to see whether the new expense is more or less in line with previous spending. If the judge rules that a private school is a necessary and reasonable expense you will be ordered to pay a share.

The judge will also look at the child's special needs, and even if you were not paying for private schooling prior to separation, if a need arises for the child to go to private school, you may well be ordered to pay your share of this.

Payments to the Child

Even if you have an adult child, payments must go to the other parent. Giving money directly to your child, no matter how generous, will not reduce your child support obligation.

Previous Relations and Child Support Payments

There are no specific rules in the Child Support Guidelines for child support payments to be adjusted because of a second, pre-existing child support order.

For example, you cannot deduct the child support you are paying your first ex-spouse from the total income you use in determining how much child support you will pay in your new child support order.

However, when application is made to the court for child support you can claim that the payments called for by the Child Support Guidelines, when combined with the child support you are already paying, causes an "undue hardship."

The undue hardship section of the guidelines contain a subsection that says undue hardship may occur when "the spouse has a legal duty under a judgment, order or written separation agreement to support any person."

However, a reduction in your payments because of your child support payments is not automatic. When ruling whether child support payments cause undue hardship, the judge will examine the standard of living in each household.

If your standard of living is not lower than that of your second ex-spouse, your request to have your payments reduced will be denied.

Food and Clothing Credit

Because you have no control over how your child support payments are used by the other parent, no credit will be applied against your child support payments for purchasing food and clothing for your children.

The reason for this rule is that while you may feel that new clothes are a priority for your child, the other parent may have already budgeted money for groceries or daycare. Basically any purchases of food and clothing for your children, whether they are during your visitations or while the child is in the custody of the other parent, are your choice – but your child support payments are your duty.

Unmatched Parental Income

In determining child support, the federal guidelines operate under the basic assumption that parents should direct the same proportion of their income towards the care of their children as they would if the couple was still together. This means that even if the custodial parent earns more than the non-custodial parent child support is still payable.

Undue Hardship

Undue hardship refers to the situation that occurs when child support payments cause serious financial difficulties to the payor.

To determine whether either party is experiencing financial hardship, the judge looks at two separate criteria:

1. Determine whether the parent "has a case"; that is, whether they will actually have difficulties supporting the child or paying the child support

2. Compare the standard of living in both households to see whether there is a disparity between the two. The guidelines set out a complicated test that helps to compare these standards of living. The test takes into account the incomes of every member of each household to determine whether one household is significantly better off than the other.

What this two-step process does is investigate the living circumstances of both households. The guidelines set out the following instances where undue hardship may be claimed:

- The spouse has responsibility for an unusually high level of debts reasonably incurred to support the spouses and their children prior to the separation or to earn a living
- The spouse has unusually high expenses in relation to exercising access to a child
- The spouse has a legal duty under a judgment, order or written separation agreement to support any person
- The spouse has a legal duty to support a child, other than a child of the marriage, who is
  - under the age of majority, or
  - the age of majority or over but is unable, by reason of illness, disability or other cause, to obtain the necessaries of life; and
- The spouse has a legal duty to support any person who is unable to obtain the necessaries of life due to an illness or disability. If your situation falls into any one (or more) of these five categories then a claim for undue hardship may be successful.

Cost of Child Support

If you are able to prove a situation of undue hardship, the court will determine how much child support you will have to pay. This figure will be based on the judge's comparison of the two household standards of living.

Additionally, the judge will take into account any other financial obligations that may interfere with your ability to meet your child support payments. The court may specify that after a reasonable time has passed to allow you to pay off any onerous debts, you will resume paying the amount of child support ordered before the undue hardship claim was made.

If so, you may be able to petition the court after that time has passed to re-examine whether the undue hardship still exists.

Overseas Calculations

If you live in a foreign country and are paying child support to a former partner in Canada, your child support is calculated as though you lived in Canada. This means that your child support will be based on the tables in the federal Child Support Guidelines for the province in which your children reside.

While these vary from province to province, there are reciprocating agreements between Canadian jurisdictions and countries on all five continents. If you live in a reciprocating jurisdiction, your support order will be registered with that country's courts, and will be enforced as rigidly as one ordered within the country.

Taxes and Cost of Living

If you live in a different country where taxes and the cost of living are much higher than they are in Canada, unfortunately, there are no specific provisions in the Child Support Guidelines that reduce child support payments in your case.

In fact, Section 19 of the guidelines provides for support to be increased if the payor lives in a country with "significantly lower" tax rates.

Child Support for Adult Children

If you are paying child support for an adult child who has left home to attend school, the amount of child support payable is left to the judge's discretion. However, there are generally two different ways that child support payments are calculated in this situation.

The first is that you may be required simply to pay the amount shown in the table for your child, plus your share of a limited amount of the child's expenses – normally, tuition, textbooks and residence.

The other method of calculation is to prepare a budget for all of the child's living expense when away from home. This would include not only tuition, textbooks and residence, but all food, travel expenses, and more. You and the other parent would share the payment of this budget in proportion to your incomes. In addition to this, you'd be required to pay a fixed monthly amount, often half of the table amount of child support, to cover the other parent's fixed expenses, such as the child living there during holidays and the summer, as well as maintaining a house year round that's large enough to accommodate the child.

Determining Income

This chapter is one close to everyone's heart, and pocketbook. I will walk you through some very important questions to help put you at ease and educate you on your rights and obligations.

Income for Child Support

Your income for child support purposes is most often equal to the "Total Income" you entered on line 150 of your T1 General income tax form. However, this figure is subject to modification in a number of specific cases.

One case occurs in the event of "non-recurring" business losses or capital losses. This rule is to prevent payers from inflating their losses in order to avoid paying higher child support. These amounts are normally added back to your income for determining what income should be used to calculate child support.

Similarly, "non-recurring" income is often not included in your income for determining the amount of child support you should pay. For instance, if you cash in an RRSP, this is income that you must include on your tax return. However, normally, this amount won't be considered when determining your income for child support purposes.

The exercise of stock options received through employment is a bit more difficult and complicated, and may or may be included in your income for child support circumstances, depending on the exact provisions of your compensation arrangement with your employer.

If you're self-employed, there will be an attempt to determine what your "true" income is rather than using your income for tax purposes. This is because often self-employed people structure there compensation in ways that are advantageous for tax purposes, but don't properly reflect the income they have available to help their children.

So, for instance, if you are self-employed and you are leaving money in your corporation each year to reduce taxes, the money you leave in your corporation may be included in your income for purposes of determining the amount of child support you should pay. Similarly, if you are deducting home office expenses, these amount may be added back to your income for the purpose of calculating child support.

The judge will also consider amounts the corporation pays to people at non-arm's length (such as family and friends) and how these amounts affect the corporation's pre-tax income.

There is a section of the Child Support Guidelines that provides the judge with powers to "impute" income to a spouse in several different cases. These include when that spouse is exempt from federal and provincial income tax, as well as non-residents who live in countries with lower income tax rates than Canada's.

A judge can also impute income when a spouse is (or is thought to be) hiding income, is intentionally unemployed or under-employed, or receives a majority of income that is taxable at lower rates, such as dividends or capital gains.

Judges are also given broad power to decide whether expenses deducted from income are "reasonable." This power allows them to disregard expenses, even if they are considered legal under Canada's Income Tax Act.

Judges can also examine the payer's income over the past three years to determine a "pattern of income." From this pattern, the judge can set the payer's income at any level deemed reasonable to account for any fluctuations that seem out of place.

Self-Employment

If an individual is self employed, his or her income is still considered to be the amount entered on Line 150 of their federal income tax return. However, the reasonableness of that income is determined by the court, which examines the individual's company financial statements for the past three years.

In this examination, the court will be checking to see if the expenses claimed by the business are reasonable, and will also be carefully examining any payments made by the company to employees, contractors, or consultants who are not at "arm's length" to ensure these payments are reasonable.

If an individual is self employed but is involved in a partnership, the court will also examine information related to how much money the person has drawn off the partnership in salary for the past three years.

If this amount is found to be too low when compared with the income of the partnership, the judge may impute income to the individual.

Low Paying Job

The federal Child Support Guidelines include provisions that allow judges to examine cases where a spouse is (or is considered to be) deliberately unemployed or underemployed to avoid a child support obligation.

If this situation occurs when you and your spouse are still finalizing the support order, you should make sure to request that the court examine your spouse's pattern of income from the past three years to see if his or her new job status is unreasonable given their earning potential.

You can also petition the court to re-examine your spouse's income pattern at any point during the duration of the order. If the court finds that your ex-spouse or partner has quit or deliberately become underemployed to avoid a child support obligation, it has some power to act to ensure your child support will be reasonable.

The court can impute an income that it considers appropriate to your ex-spouse and then require her or him to pay child support commensurate to that income.

Income Fluctuations

If your income fluctuates, you can request that the court examine your income carefully to determine a reasonable average income, which can then be used along with the Child Support Guidelines tables to provide an appropriate child support figure.

The court will examine your income tax returns (and any other documentation and financial records it deems appropriate) to determine a pattern of income. Additionally, this will help account for any major fluctuations that may occur from year to year.

Overtime and Bonuses

Generally, overtime is included on your T4 and entered on line 101 of your T1 General federal income tax return. As such, it is definitely included in your calculation of income.

However, if you received more overtime in a single year only (due to company restructuring or a labour shortage, for example) you do not have to worry about being assessed an unreasonable amount of child support.

In such a case, you can request that the court examine your pattern of income over the past three years to ensure that the income used for calculating your support payments is not too far off of your usual income.

Capital Gains and Losses

Capital gains are usually treated as income for child support purposes. However, if you have a number of capital gains and losses throughout the year, you are allowed to deduct the capital losses from the gains. Because capital gains and losses are treated differently for tax purposes, you are required to submit the actual capital gain (rather than the taxable capital gain), less the actual capital losses you have experienced.

The court will likely want to examine your financial records, as well as any applicable documentation, to ensure that the capital gains and losses are reasonable.

Large – One-Time Capital Gain

Although it is possible to exempt all or part of a one-time capital gain from federal income tax, you still have to include this capital gain as income when calculating your child support.

However, you can petition the court to consider your pattern of income for the past three years, so you can show that the capital gain was a one-time opportunity.

The income pattern provision of the Child Support Guidelines does specify that the judge will consider non-recurring sources of income in determining your income for child support calculations.

Remarriage

If you are involved in a new relationship, you do not have to fear paying more child support based on your new spouse's income, unless your current child support order includes an "undue hardship" provision. Your child support obligation is based on your income alone.

However, if you claimed and were granted relief on your payments because they created undue financial hardship, your ex-spouse or partner could petition the court to have your child support order re-examined if you get involved in a new relationship.

If this re-examination occurs, the court will compare the standard of living of both households, including the income of both spouses. The court will be looking to determine whether your household still has a significantly lower standard of living than your ex-spouse's.

Therefore, the examination will look at the total household income of both spouses, as well as the number of children and other obligations in each household. Thus, while the amount of your child support will be based on your income alone, whether or not you receive any relief from these payments is based on your income and your new spouse's combined.

Earning Power versus Actual Earning

Yes, the court can consider a spouse's income earning potential when determining the amount of child support you are required to pay. The Child Support Guidelines allow the court to impute (assign) income to you if it determines that you are intentionally unemployed or underemployed.

However, if you can prove you have done so in order to help care for any of your children (whether they are covered by the child support order or not) the court will generally not impute income to you.

Adult Children

Most people think of child support in relationship to smaller children. However, as you will see in this chapter, child support often goes beyond the teen years.

COLLEGE / UNIVERSITY AGE

If your child is attending post-secondary education, the Child Support Guidelines include provisions that could continue your child support payments.

Normally, child support continues until your child has completed his or her first post-secondary degree. However, this is not an absolute limit. There have been recent cases which require parents to pay child support for longer periods of time. This normally happens where the parents themselves have an extensive post-secondary education – for instance, a physician may be ordered to pay child support for a child in medical school.

Amounts Paid

The court will examine the incomes of both parents, as well as any earnings by the adult child, when determining what it considers an appropriate amount of child support.

In doing so, it will consider the financial ability of both parents to contribute to the child's education, and it will also consider the financial ability of the child. If your child earns enough to pay for his or her education, you may not be required to contribute at all. Obviously, given the costs of university today, this is not a likely scenario.

The court has broad discretion in setting what it feels is an appropriate amount to further the child's education. It will take into consideration not only the basic support needed to sustain a reasonable quality of life for your child, but also special expenses such as tuition and books.

If your child is still living at home with the custodial parent, child support will often simply be calculated as if your child were under 18.

If your child is attending university or college in a different city from the custodial parent, you will be required to pay a portion of the child's expenses – including tuition, textbooks and residence.

Child's Income

If your child support order comes before the courts for consideration, the adult child's income will be considered along with that of both parents when determining how much child support you will be required to pay.

The resulting order will take into account the ability of all parties to contribute financially. It is most likely that a judge will deduct your adult child's income from the cost of the course of study, and then require you and your ex-spouse to provide proportional shares of the remainder in much the same way you shared special expenses when your child was a minor. Plus, you'll still be required to pay a monthly amount of child support on top of that.

Post-Secondary Education Expenses

The types of expenses required by post-secondary education will vary depending on the location of the school and the type of program your child has embarked on.

Tuition and books are probably the most common of these expenses. However, some programs may also require lab fees, practicum placement fees, special tools and equipment.

Other expenses may include food and lodging if the program takes your child away from home. When considering the child support order, the court will determine which of these expenses is reasonable, and also what share the payor will be required to contribute.

LACK OF COMMUNICATION

Unfortunately, in a lot of cases, there is a breakdown in the relationship between the adult child and the child support payor. However, this is normally not a ground on which you can end child support.

If you have a child that refuses to communicate with you, remember that child support is completely separate from custody or access: if you are required by a child support order to pay child support, you must continue to do so for any child covered by that order until the court tells you to stop.

The reason for this is that child support exists to ensure that children receive a fair amount of financial support from both parents throughout their young lives.

Therefore, whether your adult child communicates with you or not, you must continue to pay the child support you have been obliged to pay for the duration of your court order or agreement.

WORKING / RETURNING TO SCHOOL

Some students choose to work for awhile and then go back to school. In this scenario, there are many variables at work in determining whether child support must still be paid once the child returns to school.

The court will consider many factors, such as the age of the child, whether they are living in a committed relationship, the child's income, and the reasons for the child leaving school and returning to school.

Because one of the generally accepted times for cutting child support is after the first post-secondary degree or diploma, it is quite likely that you will be required to pay child support when your child returns to school if the interruption was for something like taking a year off to travel through Europe.

Another accepted time for terminating support is when the child is able to support himself or herself, so if your child has been out in the world for a few years, the judge may not order a resumption of support.

Stepchildren

This is another important topic, often overlooked by couples. To help clear things up, I have covered this in this chapter.

PAYING REQUIREMENTS

To the surprise of most people, stepparents may be required to pay child support for their stepchildren.

This can be true even if the child's biological father is already paying child support. In fact, it is not uncommon for the custodial payer to receive payments from more than one former spouse.

In stepparent cases, courts are given the discretion to decide how much child support should be paid. One commonly applied "rule of thumb" is to calculate how much the stepparent would be required to pay under the Child Support Guidelines, then deduct from that the amount of child support that the biological parent is paying.

If the biological parent is not paying anything (for instance, the biological parent is unemployed, ill or cannot be located), then the stepparent may be on the hook for the full table amount of child support.

A stepparent, then, may be required to pay any amount ranging from a token top-up amount to the full amount called for by the Child Support Guidelines.

DECIDING FACTORS

The test to determine whether a stepparent must pay child support is whether the stepparent has "stood in the place of a parent for the child" or as lawyers often like to say "in loco parentis." Generally, if you've lived with the children for any substantial amount of time, you're going to be on the hook for child support. However, if your had a more transient relationship, then you may not need to pay child support.

Even if your relationship with the stepchildren is strained, has broken off, or was never very strong, or even if it was the reason for you breaking up with your partner, you may well be found to have acted in loco parentis to the children. This is particularly so if you financially support the children beforehand, even in an indirect way such as making the mortgage payments.

TWO FATHERS

An interesting question asked is if a child can receive child support from two fathers? Yes, provincial legislation and the federal Child Support Guidelines allow for support to be paid by more than one parent, usually a biological parent and a step-parent. However, support may be ordered for two step-parents as well.

There is no need for the payor to be of the opposite sex, either.

Separation Agreements

As you have seen so far, there are many different things to know about child support, both from the child's and the parent's perspective.

UNDERSTANDING THE AGREEMENT

In Canada, your legal separation agreement is a contract between yourself and your ex-partner. It normally will include provisions regarding child support. Your separation agreement is a written agreement that is recognized by the courts and in fact has the force of a court order.

Acceptance by the Judge

The judge does not have to accept the child support agreement that is in your separation agreement. The judge's primary concern is to ensure that your children are provided with adequate financial funding.

If you apply for a divorce, it is from this point of view that the judge will be examining the child support section of your separation agreement. The judge will take into consideration the fact that you and your spouse did agree when making his or her determination, but the final say with regards to child support lies with the judge.

If the amount agreed on meets the federal guidelines or is higher, the judge likely will accept your child support agreement and grant you a divorce. Otherwise, there may be problems obtaining a divorce.

Differences from the Guidelines

If needed, you can make a child support agreement that is different from the guidelines. The judge will take many things under advisement when examining a child support agreement, and will base their decision on what it rules are the best interests of the child.

When approving a child support agreement a judge must consider the guidelines, but can vary from them if there is a case for undue hardship or some other specific reason for a variance.

Some examples of these specific reasons may include transfer of property or some other financial transaction that is in lieu of some child support, income in excess of $150,000, or special costs associated with visits to your child.

The judge will also take into consideration the fact that the agreement is acceptable to both payer and receiver, but he or she is charged with ensuring that the child or children receive an adequate share of the payer's income.

You can also make a child support agreement that exceeds the child support amount laid out in the guidelines. The courts are under no obligation to ensure that child support payments are not excessive.

VARYING CHILD SUPPORT

There are no circumstances under which a child support agreement is "set in stone," nor is it necessarily in your best interest to do this. Any parent can apply for variation of their child support at any time based upon a change in circumstances.

These changes can include an increase or drop in income for the payor, new needs for the child, or any number of special factors that could require that payments be either raised or lowered.

Variation of Child Support

Child support is not locked in forever. Normally, as the payor's income changes, child support changes.

LOCKED IN AGREEMENT

Regardless of whether you are the parent paying child support or the parent who is receiving child support, the answer is no, you are not stuck with your child support agreement or court order.

Either the payor or the payee may apply to the court to have your child support agreement or order changed based on a change in circumstances.

CHANGING SUPPORT

The way in which you change the child support that you are paying or receiving depends on whether or not the other parent is in agreement with making changes.

If you and your ex-partner agree, you may simply amend your existing written agreement with the new amounts or conditions. You may also amend your existing court order with the new information and then file the new order with the court.

You may want to use the guidelines to assist you in making a new agreement. The judge will then review the changes you propose and decide whether they are reasonable and still serve the best financial interests of your child or children, based on the Child Support Guidelines. The court may then accept your proposed changes or order another amount that it considers appropriate.

If you and your ex-partner do not agree to make changes then you may make an application to the court for a judge to decide on your case. The court will use the federal Child Support Guidelines to determine the appropriate amount of child support in your case. The judge will also order each party to pay their share of any necessary and reasonable special or extraordinary expenses.

RETROACTIVE SUPPORT

Although courts are hesitant to make such orders unless there is an explanation for delay, it does occur. Judges are also hesitant to order the return of money already paid.

Typically, though, you can only change child support retroactive to the date that you apply for a change, unless there is a good reason for your delay in applying. Generally, judges won't order a change in child support more than a year prior to a request for the change being made.

There is another situation that could see a retroactive change made. If your spouse consented to a retroactive change, then you could change your child support retroactively. This could occur if you have been out of contact for several months, and new expenses associated with your child has arisen.

ARREAR CALCULATIONS

Child support arrears can be divided into two categories. The first is arrears related to an existing child support agreement or court order. Any missed payments owing are considered in arrears until they are paid, regardless of how long ago the payment was missed.

Child support enforcement agencies may help you to collect the arrears. If you are a payor and would like to request relief from your arrears based on financial hardship, you must apply to have your case heard before the courts.

The second type of arrears is payments owing for a new child support order or agreement. Basically, arrears of this type make up for time lost waiting for a court to become available to review your case.

RETIREMENT

You are bound by your existing child support order or agreement until it expires or until you get a new order that reflects your changed circumstances. This means that if you retire you still have the same child support order you had before you retired.

You cannot unilaterally decide to stop paying child support or to pay less child support unless you have received permission from the courts to do so. You can go back to court to have your new income situation addressed, or you can enter a new agreement with your ex-partner based on your new situation.

If you retire for good reason and do get a new order or agreement it will be based on your pension income as well as any other sources of income – federal pension, income from your Registered Retirement Savings Plan (RRSP) pay outs, or stock options that may be exercised as a result of your retirement.

Reduction of Arrears

It is relatively rare for a court to reduce arrears of child support. However, there are a few circumstances when this might occur. The payor may at any time request a reduction of arrears based on a change of circumstances.

The wording of federal and provincial legislations governing these arrears varies, but the onus is on the payor to prove that the change of circumstances warrants the reduction or cancellation of arrears.

Judges tend to take a fairly harsh stand against payors in arrears on their child support, so payers need to be prepared to answer some difficult questions regarding their request. One of the first deals with why the payor let the arrears build up before asking for a variation in his or her payments.

If you experience a change in circumstance, then, it is a good idea to let the court know about it before you have to start missing or reducing child support payments. The payor will also be asked about any catastrophic changes such as job loss or injury that prevent him or her from earning enough to pay off their arrears.

Payors should also be prepared to discuss what efforts they have made to reduce the arrears prior to applying to the court for relief. Payors should also be prepared with a statement of all their assets, liabilities, income, and expenses to show why they are unable to pay their arrears.

Unpaid child support is considered one of the largest problems facing children in Canada and all over the world, so judges are, generally, highly reluctant to reduce arrears – so be prepared with good arguments to show why your case qualifies for relief of arrears.

REMARRIAGE

The Child Support Guidelines contain no provisions for reducing child support simply because you are remarrying. In fact, you may end up losing any "undue hardship" provisions contained in your original agreement or order, because undue hardship claims are based on a comparison of the standard of living in your home and the other parent's home.

Unfortunately, having a child support order or agreement provides you with an obligation to continue supporting your children, regardless of circumstance. This means that even if you are returning to school you will be required to comply with the terms of your child support order or agreement and continue paying child support.

There are no circumstances under which you can unilaterally decide to stop paying child support. However, the Child Support Guidelines allow for variations to be granted when there is a significant change in the circumstances of the payor.

If you would like to request a temporary variation in your child support payments to return to school, you must first consult a court and/or discuss the matter with your former spouse.

Your request will have a better chance for success if the educational program you are planning to attend will significantly improve your earning power. When you are preparing your request, be sure to highlight the benefits your new education will hold for your children, whether these benefits are financial or will help improve your parent-child relationship.

Your chances will also be increased if you can show that you are re-training for a new career, or that you have been laid-off or "downsized" and need to find a new career path.

Ultimately, your child support order may prevent you from returning to school, unless you can find a way to continue to meet your child support obligations. While it is unfortunate that child support can prevent you from making choices in life, the Child Support Guidelines are clear that it is your responsibility to continue paying child support until a court says that you do not have to.

If the judge finds that your request for a variation is not reasonable, you may have to put off your return to school until you are able to pay for both your education and child support.

LAYOFF

If you have experienced a significant drop in earnings, you can apply for a variation of your child support order or agreement based on your new income. However, until you apply to the court for this variation you will still be required to pay the amount of child support contained in the original child support order or agreement.

When examining your request for a variation, the court will consider the circumstances of your job loss (i.e. if you have been "downsized" rather than fired for cause). The court will likely grant a variation, at least for a short time.

The judge will expect you to look for another job with earnings consistent with your pattern of earnings for the previous three years. If you take a lower paying job than you are qualified for you will likely have to justify your choice to a judge. If your explanation is unsatisfactory, however, the judge can order you to resume paying the amount called for in your original child support order or agreement.

WAGE GARNISHMENT

Notifying the Family Responsibility Office that your income has changed won't be helpful. You need to remember that this is simply an enforcement agency.

In other words, they can only enforce the terms and obligations of existing orders. Your current child support obligation is the amount specified in your order or agreement and it is this amount that the Family Responsibility Office is garnishing.

If your income has changed then it is up to you or your ex-partner to get a new order. This new order will then be followed by the Family Responsibility Office and the amount of child support being garnished will be in accordance with your new financial circumstances as specified in the new order.

Termination of Child Support

After years of paying child support, you have finally met your obligations. Now comes the time for termination but along with that, many questions.

ENDING TIME

In Canada child support typically is owed as long as your children are in college or university earning their first post-secondary degree or diploma.

QUITTING SCHOOL

If your child is over the age of majority and has stopped going to school but you have an order requiring child support, then you need to have the situation addressed by a judge. Until you have a new order you are bound by the terms and obligations of your existing order.

NO GRADUATION

You are required to pay child support until a judge tells you that you can stop. This may be when your child reaches the age of majority (18 or 19 depending on the province you live in) but in most cases it can be extended to assist children who are still dependent on their parents.

This category includes adult children attending school as well as children with medical needs. The expectation for child support for adult children attending school is that child support will typically be paid while your child completes high school as well as the first degree or diploma program.

Enforcement of Child Support Orders

Many people are curious as to the methods for enforcing child support payments, which is covered in this chapter.

PAYROLL DEDUCTIONS

In general, child support must go through the provincial child support agency, unless the child support payee agrees otherwise.

The provincial child support agency will then enforce child support directly, normally through payroll deductions. Given the vast numbers of people who pay child support this way, there normally is no stigma for these automatic payroll deductions occurring, especially as the choice is really in the hands of the child support payee.

If the child support payee agrees, you can opt out of the provincial enforcement scheme. Normally, you would set up automatic monthly bank transfers, or provide the child support payee with post-dated cheques for a year or so.

PAYMENT ENFORCEMENT

Child support payments are enforced by a variety of different provincial agencies created for this purpose, as follows:

- Family Responsibility Office – Ontario
- Maintenance Enforcement Agency Manitoba (charged with ensuring child support payments are made)
- Maintenance Enforcement Agency - Yukon, Prince Edward Island, Northwest Territories, and Nova Scotia
- B.C.'s Family Maintenance Enforcement Program – West Region
- Maintenance Enforcement Program – Alberta and Saskatchewan
- Support-Payment Collection Program – Quebec
- Nunavut Court of Justice - Canada's newest territory
- Family Support Orders Service – New Brunswick
- Support Enforcement Division - Newfoundland and Labrador

Each of these agencies has broad powers to compel payors to meet their child support obligations, which vary from province to province. These powers may include the ability to garnish wages to receive child support payments, arrears, and interest.

The agency may also be able to suspend the payor's driver's licence or passport and go directly to the federal government to garnish federal payments such as income tax refunds, Employment Insurance and the GST/HST Credit.

Agencies can also seize bank accounts and assets, and report payors to credit bureaus in order to have this reflected on their credit rating. These agencies also have the power to charge fees for a number of their services.

These fees can include charges for post-dated or N.S.F. cheques, adjustments to payor's accounts due to payments, which bypass the enforcement agency and charges for letters and other documents requested.

COLLECTING OUTSIDE CANADA

If the other parent lives outside of Canada you can have your child support order enforced by contacting the provincial agency responsible for enforcing child support orders, provided the other parent lives in a country that has a reciprocal agreement with your province.

If your former spouse lives in a reciprocating jurisdiction, your provincial agency will contact the enforcement agency in that country, which will then work to enforce the child support order.

Once your provincial agency has contacted the reciprocal jurisdiction, the child support order is usually treated by that country as though it were ordered in that jurisdiction. This means that the reciprocating jurisdiction will be able to use any means legally at its disposal to ensure that your former spouse fulfils their child support obligation.

Thus, the degree of enforcement may be slightly stronger (or weaker) than if your spouse were living in Canada. It is not required that you work through an enforcement agency to collect child support from a parent living abroad, but this is normally the only cost-effective way to proceed.

FAMILY RESPONSIBILITY OFFICE

The Family Responsibility Office is a branch of the province of Ontario's Ministry of Community and Social Services. Its function is to ensure that child support is payments pass from the paying parent to the receiving parent.

The Family Responsibility Office operates under the authority of the Family Responsibility and Support Arrears Act, 1986. The Family Responsibility Office receives every child support order made by the provincial and federal courts of Ontario.

These include orders made by a judge and orders that result from private written agreements that include terms of child support and that are filed with the family court.

The Family Responsibility Office enforces payments of the amounts of child support made in these orders and agreements. The Family Responsibility Office has the authority to receive child support payments and arrear payments and to make payment agreements with the parents ordered to pay child support.

When a case is registered with the Family Responsibility Office, the parent paying child support makes payments to the Family Responsibility Office. This is usually done through direct payroll or other income deductions, but can be done through direct payment to the Family Responsibility Office.

When the Family Responsibility Office receives these payments, they then pass the support on to the receiving parent.

Enforcing Support

The Family Responsibility Office enforces child support in a number of ways. Initially, child support obligations are enforced by deducting the amount owed from the paying parent's wage or source of income.

This is done by sending a notice to the paying parent's employer or the source of their income advising them that they need to begin making deductions. The employer or income source is required by law to make these deductions from the paying parent's income when they receive this notification. A copy of this notice is also provided to the paying parent.

If you are self employed or do not have a steady income source the Family Responsibility Office enforces your child support order by requiring you to make direct payments to their office. They provide a number of options for payment.

If the paying parent does not meet their child support obligations then the Family Responsibility Office can take action under the Family Responsibility and Support Arrears Enforcement Act, 1996. These actions include garnishing federal funds (EI, Income Tax, GST), and suspending licenses (federal, driver's license) and passports.

Bypassing the Agency

The Family Responsibility Office can be bypassed if both parents agree to make payments privately and directly from the payor to the recipient. This agreement needs to be made in writing if you are to withdraw from the Family Responsibility Office programs. There is a special "Notice of Withdrawal" form that both parents must complete and forward to the Family Responsibility Office.

WAGE GARNISHMENT

Should you go through the provincial enforcement agency, or elect to receive child support payments directly? There are several benefits to going through the provincial enforcement agency.

The first benefit is the reliability of the timing of child support payments – instead of receiving payments when the other parent chooses to make them, you can receive money on a regular basis. This can ensure a steady cash flow.

Another advantage is to ensure that your spouse make the child support payments, which provides an element of certainty.

If you have an amicable relationship with the other parent, or at least trust them, then obviously these benefits don't mean much, and it probably doesn't make sense to go through your provincial enforcement agency.

The main disadvantage of going through your provincial enforcement agency is the normal disadvantages of large bureaucracies. Normally, the provincial enforcement agencies are slow and inefficient. Even if the other parent cooperates with them completely, you may need to wait 3 or 4 months before you receive your first child support payment.

INTEREST ON UNPAID SUPPORT

Normally, a court order will include a provision regarding interest on unpaid amounts of child support. Similarly, many separation agreements will also contain such a provision.

In Ontario, the Family Responsibility Office will enforce interest on support payments when the interest rate is stated in the court order or agreement.

Document Disclosure

One of the most cumbersome aspects of child support, regardless of parent, is the documentation required. However, in this chapter, we have outlined some information to make the process easier.

NORMAL DOCUMENTATION

In child support cases it is normal for both the paying spouse and the custodial parent to have to disclose their federal personal income tax returns for each of the three most recent taxation years.

Along with tax returns, they should also submit all notices of assessment and reassessment issued for those three taxation years. In addition, each spouse will be required to disclose copies of their three most recent pay stubs (if they are employees), so long as this statement shows that person's total income in the year to date.

Each spouse will also be required to submit statements or letters showing totals for the year to date from any benefits received. These benefits may include: employment insurance, social assistance, a pension, workers compensation, disability payments or any other source of additional income.

The information submitted by the payor will be used to determine the amount of child support required under the Child Support Guidelines, as well as their share of any special and extraordinary expenses.

The information provided by the receiving parent will be used to determine what each spouse's share of these special expenses will be. Each spouse will be required to submit additional documentation if they are: self-employed, involved in a partnership, in control of a corporation, or the beneficiary of a trust.

SELF-EMPLOYMENT DOCUMENTATION

Self-employed spouses need to submit financial statements from their partnership, professional practice, or business for the last three taxation years.

These statements need to show both the gross income of the enterprise as well as the amount the spouse has drawn from the entity as salary for those three years. They should also disclose all expenses claimed.

Self-employed spouses are also required to submit information regarding any expense, salaries, or other payments made to parties who are considered to be not at arm's length in relation to that spouse. Parties not at arm's length may include family members, new spouses, friends, or any other person with whom the spouse has a personal relationship.

To satisfy the requirements of the Child Support Guidelines, the spouse should supply a statement detailing the amounts and reasons for these payments; the judge will examine this statement to ensure that all payments are reasonable.

NONDISCLOSURE

If your former spouse is refusing to comply with the requirements for document disclosure in the Child Support Guidelines you have several options for recourse.

You can ask the court to determine child support without the documentation, and ask the judge to make a finding that the support payor is earning more than he claims and that is why the payor is withholding financial documentation.

You can also ask the court to make an order that the other parent produce the required documentation. Refusing to produce the documentation after this is quite serious – it's considered contempt of court, and is quasi-criminal in nature. Courts don't like their own orders being disobeyed.

In any of the above instances, the judge can order the withholding spouse to pay some or all of the legal costs of the other spouse up to the full amount incurred.

Miscellaneous Child Support Issues

In this chapter, I hit on a few things that did not fit into other mentioned categories.

NEW DISCOVERY

What happens when a man discovers that a long-time girlfriend had his child – is he responsible for child support retroactively or just currently since he was not even aware he was a father?

A court will not typically order child support beyond the date your ex-girlfriend applied for it. This means that the date your girlfriend made the application is likely the date of which the judge will tell you child support starts.

The exception to this would be if the judge made a finding that you had been responsible in some way for the delay in your girlfriend filing an application for child support.

BANKRUPTCY

Bankruptcy has absolutely no effect on child support payments – they will remain in full force throughout your bankruptcy. This means that you will have to continue paying your child support obligations, often before paying off any creditors who have sought action against you.

While many payors have argued that bankruptcy causes an undue hardship and affects their ability to pay child support, most courts have taken the opposite view.

Because bankruptcy eliminates your unsecured debts, the court may hold that you actually have more money available to pay your child support and will thus reject your undue hardship claim, or your claim for a rescission of arrears of child support.

Child support arrears are not erased by bankruptcy. Your arrears will be given a "preferred claim" during bankruptcy proceedings, however.

LEGAL FEES

Some legal fees for child support cases are tax deductible and some are not. Canada Revenue Agency (CRA) rules regarding legal and accounting fees (IT-99R5) state that legal costs for establishing a child support order are tax deductible for the payee.

The claimant must, however, deduct any legal costs awarded by the court from the total amount before claiming a tax deduction; in other words, you can only claim what you actually paid rather than the total amount your lawyer billed you.

Payors generally cannot claim legal fees for anything. CCRA rules prevent payors from claiming legal fees for contesting or negotiating support order. They also exclude deductions for legal fees incurred terminating or reducing child support payments.

INTERIM CHILD SUPPORT

An interim child support order is an order for child support that is made by the judge on a motion, or at least on a temporary basis until a final decision or agreement can be reached regarding child support.

The financial obligations of your interim order remain in place until you get a final order. The Divorce Act specifies that:

> "The court may make an interim order under subsection (2) for a definite or indefinite period or until a specified event occurs, and may impose terms, conditions, or restrictions in connection with the order or interim order, as it thinks fit and just.

What this says is that the judge can grant an interim order pending the completion of your court case at trial or by settlement.

www.ingramcontent.com/pod-product-compliance
Lightning Source LLC
Chambersburg PA
CBHW061239180526
45170CB00003B/1361